Where's Mom's Hair?

A Family's Journey through Cancer

By Debbie Watters, with Haydn and Emmett Watters
Photographs by Sophie Hogan

Second Story Press

Garfield County Libraries
Parachute Branch Library
244 Grand Valley Way
Parachute, CO 81635
(970) 285-9870 Fax (970) 285-7477
www.garfieldlibraries.org

DISCARDED FROM
GARFIELD COUNTY PUBLIC
LIBRARY SYSTEM

BREAST
CANCER
SOCIETY
of Canada

This is our family. Our mom got cancer and she had to have an operation. We went to visit her at the hospital every day. We liked the elevator and the snack bar! After she came home, she had to take medicine that would make all her hair fall out. We felt down, down in the dumps. So we decided to have a party, a hair-cutting party...

A lot of Mom and Dad's friends came to the party. Everyone was happy to be there, and we were happy they were there too.

We played Mom's favorite songs, and soon we were ready for the main event!

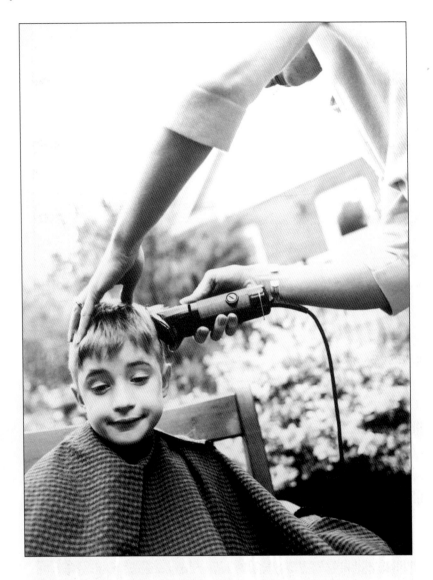

Our friend Catherine is a hairdresser and she brought her clippers. We went first. We needed our summer haircuts anyway.

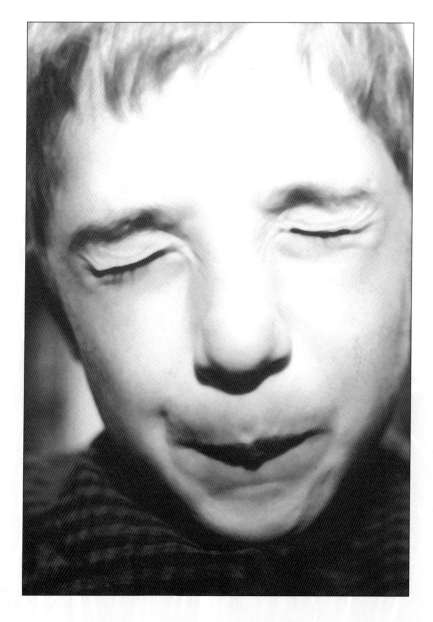

Have you ever had a brush cut? The clippers feel like a bunch of bees buzzing on your head!

Then it was Mom's turn. Her hair was coming out already, all by itself.
Mom felt really happy that she still had some hair left to cut.

Mom told all her friends that she was proud they could share this moment with her. She told us to take one last look at her hairy head.

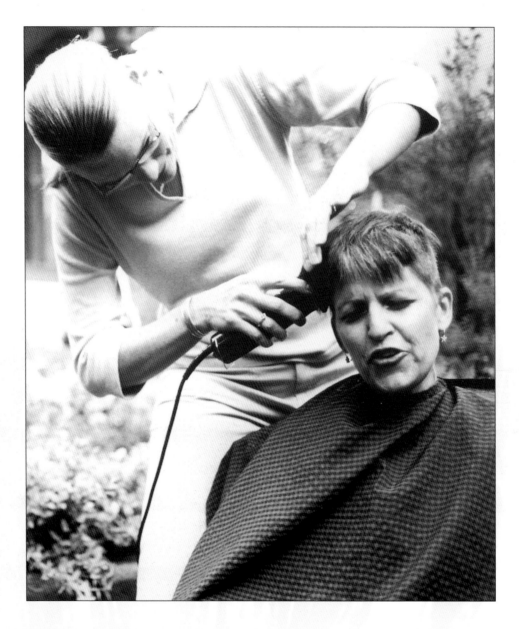

Catherine started to clip. Mom didn't seem to mind too much about the buzzing.

Look at our faces. Some of us are laughing and smiling. Some of us look sad and serious. You just don't know how you are going to feel when someone you love is losing their hair because of cancer.

Catherine clipped and clipped and clipped, until Mom's hair was very, very short. We decided to leave it like that and let the rest fall out later.

When Mom was done, she stood up. Everybody gathered around her in a circle again, but this time it was to rub her head! Her hair was so short it felt prickly. So prickly we thought we might get a hair sliver!

Mom had never had her hair so short. Soon it would be all gone, but with or without hair she was still our mom.

At the last minute Dad went under the clippers too! We all did it for Mom.

If she could do it, so could we. Now we were one big prickly-headed family!

We decided to leave the hair in the backyard so the birds could use it to build their nests, but not until we made some mustaches!

The medicine that made Mom's hair fall out is called chemotherapy (Key-mow-ther-a-pee), but we call it chemo for short. It's a special medicine that fights to destroy the cancer. She had to visit the hospital to get chemo, and she also took pills at home.

Dad and Mom's friends took her for chemo. She would relax in the waiting room until the nurse called her name.

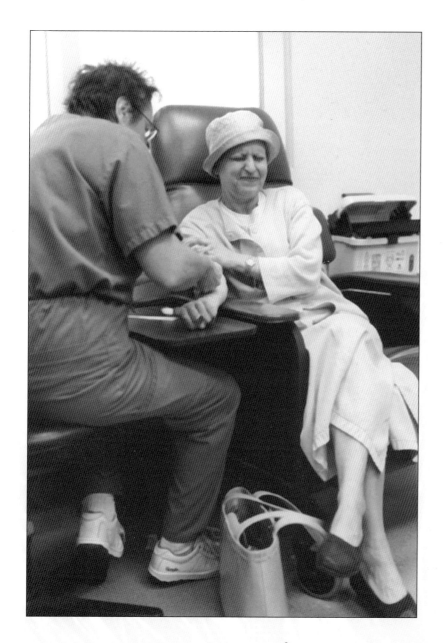 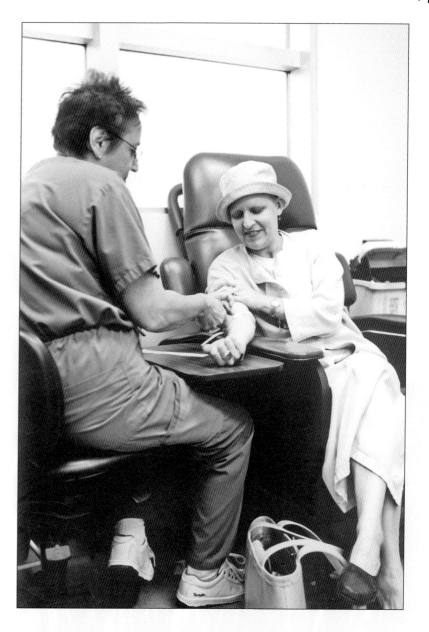

First she had her blood taken. The needle pinched, but only for a minute.

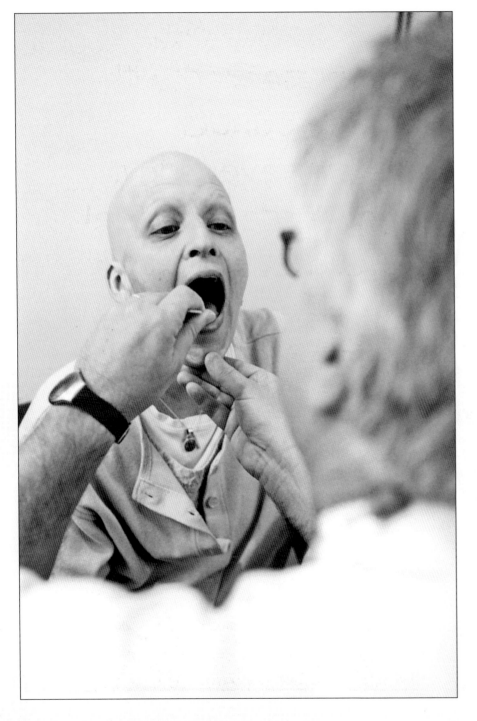

Then Mom had to talk to the doctor and the nurse. They would ask her how she was feeling and give her a checkup. A doctor who looks after cancer patients is called an oncologist (on-kol-o-jist).

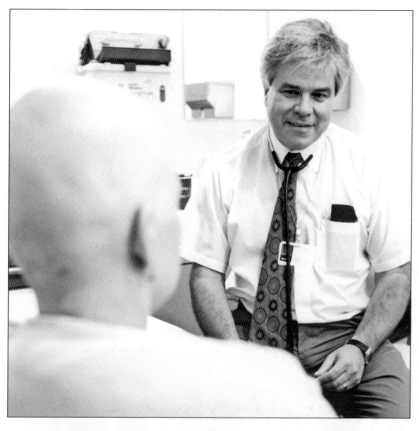

Mom's oncologist and nurse work with a lot of cancer patients every day. They made Mom feel safe. They always took very good care of her.

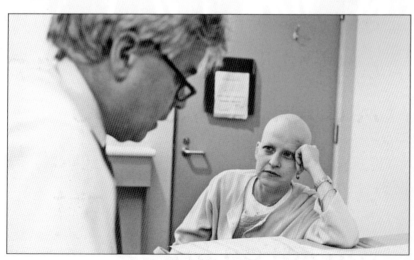

The chemo nurse used a needle to put the medicine in. The medicine made Mom feel really tired and sick. Mom said, "Sometimes you need to feel worse before you can get better."

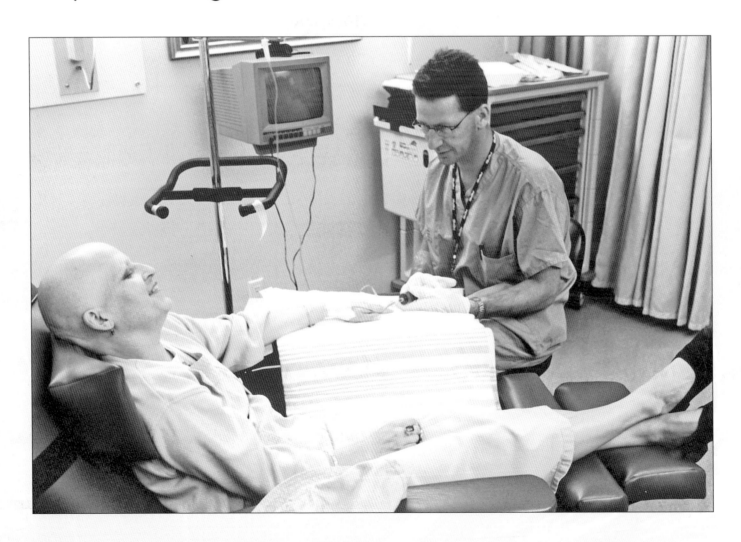

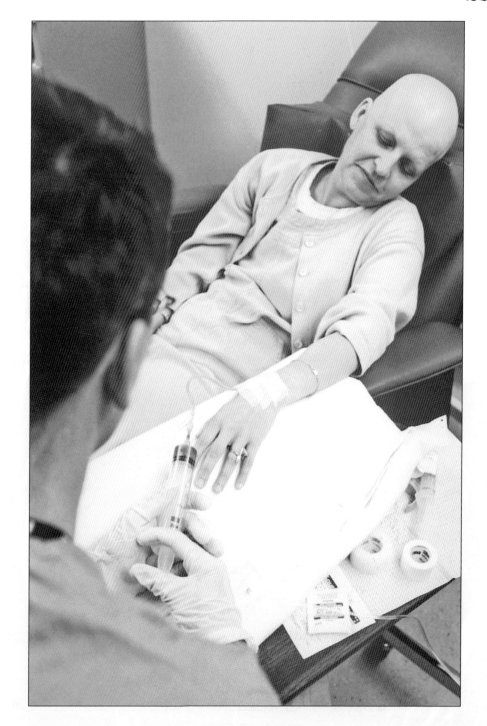

Dad was sad to see her so tired. He told us that Mom was very brave.

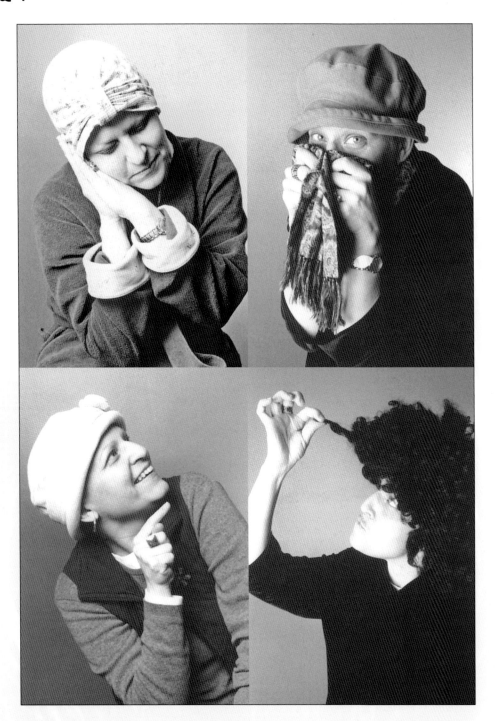

Now that Mom
was bald...

...she could dress up with wigs, hats and scarves!

And sometimes...

...we like to dress up too.

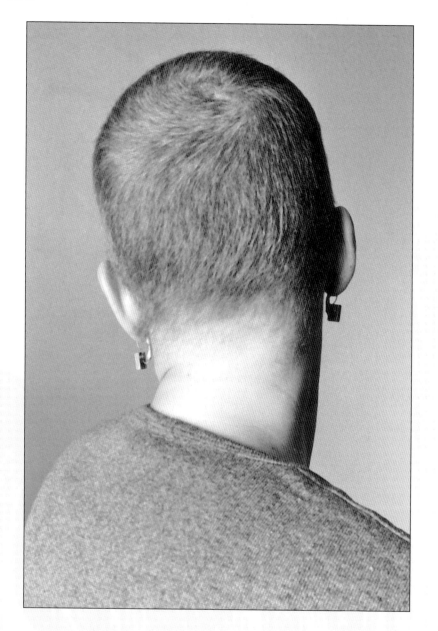 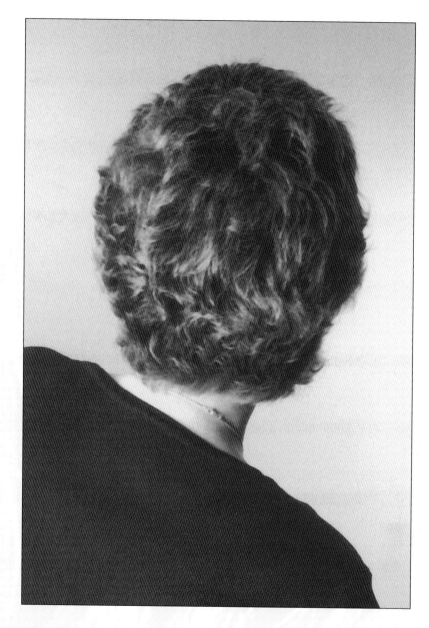

You know what's amazing? Mom's hair started to grow back even before the chemo was done.

It grew and grew and grew, until she had a whole field of hair!

When Mom's hair grew back, we had another party.
It was a hair-growing-back party, and it was FUN.
We invited all the friends who had helped us when
Mom had chemo. Everyone at the party had to wear
a hat or a wig, except Mom – she was so proud of her
new hair!

This is our family.
Mom got cancer.
We made it through
the operation.
We made it through
chemotherapy.
We made it through
Mom going bald.
We all did it together,
and now Mom has
her beautiful hair
again!

To all our family and friends who so willingly took the journey with us,
and to Shawn, a great husband and Dad.
– Debbie and the Boys.

I dedicate this book to all the Fairy Godmothers who keep memories alive.
– Sophie Hogan

Library and Archives Canada Cataloguing in Publication

Watters, Debbie, 1961-
Where's Mom's hair? : a family's journey through cancer / by Debbie Watters ;
with Haydn and Emmett Watters ; photographs by Sophie Hogan.

ISBN 1-896764-94-0

1. Watters, Debbie, 1961- --Juvenile literature. 2. Watters, Haydn--Juvenile literature.
3. Watters, Emmett--Juvenile literature. 4. Cancer--Chemotherapy--Juvenile literature. 5. Cancer--Patients--
Family relationships--Juvenile literature. 6. Cancer--Juvenile literature.

I. Watters, Haydn II. Watters, Emmett III. Hogan, Sophie IV. Title.

RC264.W38 2005   j362.196'994   C2005-900421-5

Copyright © 2005 Debbie Watters / Photographs © 2005 Sophie Hogan

Third Printing 2007

Designed by P. Rutter

Second Story Press gratefully acknowledges the support of the Ontario Arts Council and the Canada Council
for the Arts for our publishing program. We acknowledge the financial support of the Government of Canada
through the Book Publishing Industry Development Program, and the Government of Ontario through the
Ontario Media Development Corporation.

ONTARIO ARTS COUNCIL
CONSEIL DES ARTS DE L'ONTARIO

Canada Council   Conseil des Arts
for the Arts   du Canada

Published by
SECOND STORY PRESS
20 Maud Street, Suite 401
Toronto, Ontario, Canada
M5V 2M5

www.secondstorypress.on.ca